Spoilt for choice! Sam Earl's refreshment stall, about 1900.

SOFT DRINKS
Their origins and history

Col

Shire Publications Ltd

CONTENTS

Printed in Great Britain by C. I. Thomas & Sons (Haverfordwest) Ltd, Press Buildings, Merlins Bridge, Haverfordwest, Dyfed SA61 1XF.

British Library Cataloguing in Publication Data: Emmins, Colin. Soft drinks: their origins and history. 1. Non-alcoholic drinks, history. I. Title. 641.26. ISBN 0-7478-0125-8.

ACKNOWLEDGEMENTS

Illustrations are acknowledged as follows: A. G. Barr plc, page 27 (top left); Bass Museum of Brewing, Burton upon Trent, pages 1, 10 (top), 18, 23, 26 and 28; Bath Industrial Heritage Trust Limited, pages 19 (bottom) and 32; Beamish the North of England Open Air Museum, page 21 (bottom); Cheltenham Art Gallery and Museums, page 7; Dayla Soft Drinks (Southern) Limited, pages 15 (top), 22 and 29 (top right); courtesy of the Dickens House, London, page 11; Evening Standard Company Limited, page 27 (bottom); Greater London Photograph Library, page 15 (bottom); Guildhall Library, London, page 13; History of Advertising Trust, page 16 (bottom right); Hulton-Deutsch Collection, page 5; Trustees of the Imperial War Museum, page 24; R. W. Malster, pages 21 (top right) and 20 (bottom); National Portrait Gallery, London, page 8 (above); Newport Museum and Art Gallery Collections, page 21 (top left); Royal Pavilion, Art Gallery and Museums, Brighton, page 10 (bottom); Schweppes Limited, pages 9 (bottom), 12, 17 (top left) and 29 (top left); Benjamin Shaw and Sons Limited, pages 29 (bottom), 30 and 31 (top); John Topham Picture Library, pages 2 and 19 (top); Tunbridge Wells Museum and Art Gallery, page 6; courtesy of the Board of Trustees of the Victoria and Albert Museum, cover and page 14 (top); Victoria Art Gallery, Bath City Council, page 3; and Winchester Museum Service Collection, page 4.

Cover: *A manservant buying lemonade for a little girl from two women at a stall c.1835.*

Below: *The aptly named Mr Philpott delivering aerated waters of his own manufacture, around 1900.*

Taking the waters: the Pump Room, Bath, 1784; watercolour by Humphry Repton.

THE DISTANT SCENE

'The four rivers of Eden were milk, water, wine and ale. Aerated waters only appeared after the Fall,' according to G. K. Chesterton. How far after he did not record.

Indeed it was not until the late eighteenth century that scientific developments enabled artificially carbonated waters to be produced and packed in commercial quantities. Nonetheless, three different sources of liquid refreshment were available well before then as the precursors of modern soft drinks. These were small beers, spa and spring waters and fruit-flavoured drinks.

The human body has a persistent need to take in liquid and it is perfectly possible to satisfy that need by drinking only pure water. But, even conceding the popularity of natural mineral waters, most people prefer to stimulate the palate with a variety of flavoured drinks.

In earlier times it could be dangerous to drink untreated water since it was so frequently contaminated. In the middle ages,

therefore, small beers were brewed for the poor: the water boiled, flavoured with common herbs or leaves – nettles, dandelions and the like – and left to ferment before the liquor was drawn off for consumption. The strength of the resulting drink would usually be low but then its purpose was not so much to inebriate as to provide more wholesome refreshment than a suspect water supply.

Nonetheless, references are frequently disparaging. Thus Shakespeare's Jack Cade said: 'I will make it a felony to drink small beer'; or Prince Hal: 'Doth it not show vilely in me to desire small beer?' But these no doubt were serious drinkers.

Small beers might well be made at home for family consumption. And when sold they would be priced as modestly as possible for those who could afford nothing stronger – hence farthing ales.

Small beers and herbal brewing continued into the eighteenth century at least, when Dr Tobias Smollett considered '...that

3

which is drank by the common people...in all the wine countries of France, is neither so strong, nourishing, nor (in my opinion) so pleasant to the taste as the small beer of England.' He then rather spoilt the effect by adding that 'for the preservation of health, and the exhilaration of the spirits, there is no beverage comparable to simple water.'

Thomas Thetcher, a contemporary of Smollett, might well have agreed had he lived. Instead his tombstone sadly records:

> Here sleeps in peace a Hampshire Grenadier,
> Who caught his death by drinking cold small beer,
> Soldiers be wise from his untimely fall
> And when ye're hot drink Strong or none at all.

When exploring New Zealand in 1773 Captain James Cook was brewing spruce beer against the scurvy. From this long tradition came the last vestiges of herbal brewing today such as dandelion and burdock and hop bitters.

Barley water was another drink from the domestic kitchen. This simple concoction of pearl barley and water was known at least as early as 1320 and seems to have survived the centuries so modestly as to excite little remark. Indeed, Thomas Fuller in the seventeenth century considered it 'an invention which found out itself, with little more than the bare joining the ingredients together'. In the next century Fanny Burney reported that George III ('Farmer George') refreshed himself with barley water as he rode home from a hard day's hunting, although his courtiers quite failed to share his enthusiasm for such innocuous refreshment in the circumstances.

'There is no beverage comparable to simple water', said Dr Smollett, and in his day spa and spring waters enjoyed a well established reputation. Spa waters, those containing curative mineral salts, were mineral waters as strictly defined. Spring waters were more likely to be valued for the exceptional purity of the source:

> 'The Malvern water', says Dr John Wall, 'Is famed for containing just nothing at all.'

Spa waters were known in Roman times

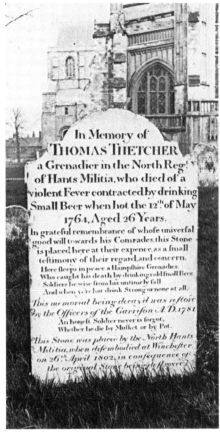

Thomas Thetcher, the Hampshire grenadier and victim of drinking cold small beer, now lies in Winchester Cathedral graveyard.

although the Romans were keener on bathing in the waters than imbibing them.

In the seventeenth century curious chemists sought to discover the composition of various mineral waters by analysis. They also found that the mineral salts could sometimes be conveniently extracted and sold as such. By 1697, for example, Dr Nehemiah Grew had analysed the composition of Epsom waters and patented his method of extracting their salts. Today magnesium sulphate is still popularly known as Epsom salts although the Epsom mineral waters have long ceased to play a part in its manufacture.

Granny was still brewing her nettle beer at Heysham, Lancashire, in 1954 — 'nettle drink' to the exciseman!

Spas developed as pleasure resorts as well as curative centres. Samuel Pepys enjoyed the social side of Epsom Spa as well as valuing the effect of the waters and half a century later Daniel Defoe found Epsom patronised more for social than medicinal reasons. The development of Bath and other spa towns is well known. But many of the old pleasure gardens of London – Sadlers Wells not least among them – adjoined springs where drinking the waters added to their attractions.

Spring waters often based their reputation on the medieval holy wells. In twelfth-century London Clerkenwell was already among the best known. In Tudor times Malvern waters were bottled and 'Some of them unto Kent; Some were to London sent: Others to Berwick went – O praise the Lord!' In the next century Tunbridge waters were bottled and corked and taken back to London.

Taking the waters: the springs at Tunbridge Wells in 1664.

By 1700, however, local competition was also to be had, to judge from an advertisement in *The Postman* which announced: 'The Chalybeate Waters at Hampstead being of the same nature and equal in virtue with Tunbridge Wells and highly approved by most of the eminent physicians of the College, as likewise by many of the gentry who formerly used to drink Tunbridge Wells waters, are by the direction of the Trustees of the Wells aforesaid, for the convenience of those who yearly drink them in London, carefully bottled in flasks and sent to Mr Philps, Apothecary, at the *Eagle and Child*, in Fleet Street every morning (for sale) at the rate of 3d per flask, and brought to persons' houses at 1d a flask more.'

In 1684 Dr Thomas Guidot suggested that the water of Sadlers Wells might be taken with a few caraway comfits, some elecampane (a form of aromatic bitters) or a little angelica. He suggested that white wine also should accompany the water and smokers were recommended to take a pipe of tobacco after drinking. A little later Dr Patrick Madan put forward similar proposals for taking the Tunbridge waters. While none of this suggests that the flavourings were mixed directly in the waters themselves, it certainly indicates an already perceived need for flavouring.

The third origin of soft drinks lay in the development of fruit-flavoured drinks. A later development than either small beers or natural waters, they nonetheless preceded the commercial soft drinks industry by at least a century. Indeed in Tudor times we find references to 'water imperial', which seems to have been a sweetened drink containing cream of tartar and flavoured with lemons, and also to 'Manays Cryste', a sweetened cordial for invalids which was flavoured with rosewater, violets or cinnamon.

At that time cordials were home-made drinks – highly flavoured, syrupy, with the consistency of a liqueur – to tempt the palate of the invalid or to be brought out on special occasions. Often more potent than officially reckoned, they might if desired be diluted to taste. They survive commercially today in essence-based peppermint,

Taking the waters: George III at Cheltenham in 1788.

ginger and clove cordials.

It was not until the reign of Charles II that fruit-flavoured drinks came into their own, as refreshment houses began to provide an alternative to taverns.

The earliest English reference to lemonade dates from the publication in 1663 of *The Parson's Wedding*, described by a friend of Samuel Pepys as 'an obscene, loose play', which had been first performed some years earlier. The drink seems to have come to England from Italy via France. Such lemonade was made from freshly squeezed lemons, sweetened with sugar or honey and diluted with water to make a still soft drink. In this guise lemonade continued through the years that followed, prepared, sold and consumed on the premises rather than bottled to take away.

In the eighteenth century Dr Samuel Johnson was among those who enjoyed lemonade and Michael Kelly, the opera singer, recalled drinking iced lemonade with a Neapolitan tavern meal in 1779.

A natural companion dating from the early eighteenth century was orangeade, for which it was found possible to use oranges too bitter to be eaten as such. Orange juice, too, came in after the Restoration, Pepys noting it with approval as a drink new to him in the 1660s.

SAILORS, SCIENTISTS AND SODA-WATER MAKERS

Fruit juices also had a medicinal value. The story of lime juice being issued to the Royal Navy to prevent scurvy and the subsequent nicknaming of British sailors as 'limeys' has been linked with Captain Cook, whom we have already noted brewing spruce beer against the same wretched disease.

We now know that the secret of citrus juices in preventing scurvy lies in their vitamin C content. Their value was remarked by Elizabethan seamen in the sixteenth century although the reason remained for

Above: *Dr Joseph Priestley (1733-1804), dissenting minister and scientist, discovered the means of artificially carbonating water.*

Below: *An early bottle of soda-water said to have been salvaged from the 'Royal George', which sank off Spithead in 1782.*

long unknown. In the mid eighteenth century James Lind proved by experiment that lemon juice cured the scurvy and Sir Joseph Banks, when travelling with Captain Cook, treated himself successfully by this means. But Cook himself was apparently unimpressed. This was almost certainly because the Admiralty, experimenting with a variety of possible cures, supplied citrus juice to him in the form of a concentrated syrup produced by boiling the juice, which was then preserved with sugar. Thus unwittingly the vital vitamin C would have been boiled away in the effort to meet the practical difficulty of keeping the juice wholesome on a long voyage.

It was not until the 1790s that the antiscorbutic virtues of lemon juice were officially recognised. Lime juice was found to keep better and to be cheaper and in the mid nineteenth century lime juice mixed with grog (rum and sugared water) became by law a part of the seaman's diet, although it was subsequently found to be less rich than lemon juice as a source of the vital vitamin.

Several scientists in the latter half of the eighteenth century interested themselves in the nature of the gas which caused certain of the spa waters to effervesce. In the late 1760s Dr Joseph Priestley, Unitarian minister and scientist, discovered a means of artificially carbonating water, which he published in 1772 as *Directions for Impregnating Water with Fixed Air*. Later, Dr John Mervyn Nooth developed an apparatus for preparing small quantities of effervescent waters and reported to that effect in the *Philosophical Transactions of the Royal Society* in 1775.

Among the claims for fixed air was that it might prove a remedy for scurvy and bottled soda-water was among the articles salvaged from the wreck of the *Royal George*, which sank off Spithead in 1782. The French scientist Antoine Lavoisier later identified fixed air as carbon dioxide.

Once the means of carbonating water was known, and the equipment for doing it was developed, the way was open for commercially manufactured soft drinks.

A Manchester apothecary, Thomas Henry, appears to have been the first maker of artificial mineral waters for sale to the public, sometime in the 1770s, by combining appropriate mineral salts, carbon dioxide gas and water. One of his successes was the commercial manufacture of an earlier concoction, Bewley's Mephitic Julep, for which the recipe required 3 drams of fossil alkali to each quart (1.1 litres) of water, and the maker was instructed to 'throw in streams of fixed air until all the alkaline taste is destroyed'. The mephitic julep was strictly medicinal and, according to Henry, effective against 'putrid fevers, scurvy, dysentry, bilious vomiting etc'. Although in those days a julep was usually a sweetened medicine, there is no suggestion that Henry's drink contained sugar.

From the beginning a successful drink depended on retaining the gas in the liquid and Henry recommended that all bottles be very closely corked and sealed. He also advised that the patient should take from 4 ounces (113 grams) at a time, 'drinking a draught of lemonade or water acidulated

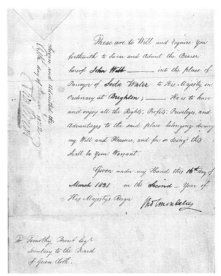

Early royal warrant for John Webb's soda-water, Brighton, 1821.

with vinegar, by which means the fixed air will be extricated in the stomach'. Again there was no suggestion of incorporating the lemonade into the mineral water.

Towards the end of the 1770s Henry was also making artificial Pyrmont and Seltzer waters. His modest commercial activities encouraged other apothecaries to make up soda-water as a sideline throughout the subsequent century.

Among the earliest soda-water makers as such were Jacob Schweppe and Nicolas Paul, partners operating in Geneva before making their separate ways to England. Schweppe set up in London in 1792 making his artificial carbonated waters on what could be called a factory scale, and Paul was operating commercially in London by 1802. It is from this period that we can more firmly date the commercial origins of soda-water, a term well established for the product by 1800.

By then soda-water had reached Dublin. There an early circular stated: 'Soda-water of single and double strength was invented by A & R Thwaites & Co in the year 1799 and introduced to the public by the late Robert Perceval Esq MD, then

Press announcement as Schweppes begin production in Bristol, 1803.

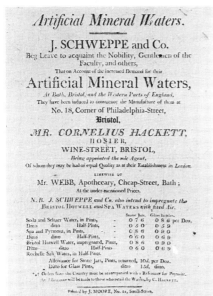

Professor of Chemistry, in his lectures in Trinity College, Dublin in 1800 since which time it has continued to receive the approbation of the medical faculty.' From the same period another Thwaites advertisement also noted 'Two shillings per dozen allowed for returned bottles', and Schweppe too provided for a returnable deposit.

The medicinal tone of soda-water continued. Advertisements in the early nineteenth century included the following: 'The Cheltenham salts, which you can procure of Mr Patheyrus, Chemist, of Bond Street, and of him alone, are to the full as efficacious and conducive to health as the water from the well.' However, the Cheltenham waters were not universally admired:

Here lies I and my three daughters,
Died from drinking the Cheltenham waters;
Had we but stuck to Epsom salts,
We wouldn't be lying in these cold vaults.

The artificial matching of spa waters probably reached its zenith in Brighton in the 1820s when Dr F. A. Struve MD opened his Royal German Spa and enabled invalids to imbibe close imitations of the Carlsbad, Marienbad, Pyrmont, Ems, Seltzer, Spa and Kissingen waters, either individually or in glorious combination, without the fatigue of crossing the Channel.

Dr F. A. Struve in fashionable silhouette at the Royal German Spa, Brighton, 1826.

Meanwhile, in verse, Lord Byron was remarking hock and soda-water as a reviver after a bout of decidedly stronger drinking.

The Royal German Spa, Brighton, about 1835.

10

FLAVOURS AND MIXERS

The origins of flavoured, artificially carbonated waters remain obscure but it was clearly some time before these early products left the chemist's shop to mingle with the more frivolous lemonades in the refreshment houses of the town.

The need for flavouring has already been remarked. Sam Weller's opinion of the waters of Bath, in Charles Dickens's *Pickwick Papers*, may be recalled: 'I thought they'd a wery strong flavour o' warm flat irons.' And Mr Smauker's retort was: 'That *is* the killybeate Mr Weller.' Chalybeate waters – 'killybeate' to Mr Smauker – were indeed distinguished by their iron salts.

The earliest reference trade historians have so far found to effervescent lemonade is in 1833, in which event the unsweetened soda-waters would have been unchallenged for over thirty years, which seems unlikely.

Ginger beer provides a link between the soda-waters on the one hand and the fruit-flavoured drinks of the commercial manu-

Ginger beer and soda-water accompany the staple products of an oyster saloon; from Dickens's 'Sketches by Boz', 1836.

facturers on the other. It seems to have had its origins among the home brews, although in Elizabethan times Barlow's *Discovery of Virginia* refers to the native Indians drinking water 'sodden with ginger in it, and black cinnamon, and some times sassafras, and divers other wholesome and medicinable herbs and trees'. However, the earliest known reference to ginger beer as such is in a *Practical Treatise on Brewing* published in 1809. By 1813 Leigh Hunt was referring to it as a drink evidently new to him and in the 1820s Charles Lamb mentioned it among the staple fare of a suburban farmhouse putting up a few light refreshments for the passing trade.

In 1819 the *Morning Chronicle* advertised: 'Pitt & Co's Ginger Beer and Soda Water. The public are most respectfully informed that they may be supplied with any quantities of these elegant and refreshing beverages at the manufactories, 17 Giltspur Street, London and 31 High Street, Lewes. The reputation attached to Pitt & Co's Ginger Beer and Soda Water renders it unnecessary to make any comment on their superiority and excellence over all others.'

At about the same time ginger beer joined the various drinkables hawked on the streets of London. Soon it was a common feature of any humble refreshment stall and among the items available for sale between the acts at the theatre.

The very close link later forged between ginger beer and schoolboy taste prompts us to ask when it was that soft drinks became particularly regarded as drinks for the young. It was not evidently in Georgian times. After dancing before George IV at Brighton, on being asked what refreshment she would like, the twelve-year-old Lady Louisa Russell requested ham sandwiches and a glass of port wine negus.

In the 1830s the boys of Rugby School were still supplied with beer as part of their staple diet because the water was considered unsafe for drinking. Or there was liquorice-water: a half-pennyworth of liquorice and the same amount of brown sugar, topped up with water and shaken with vigour.

Handbill announcing Schweppes' contract to supply refreshments to the Great Exhibition (the 'Crystal Palace'), Hyde Park, London, 1851.

Well before the end of the nineteenth century, however, Jerome K. Jerome considered that the hungry boy's idea of a square meal would include a bottle of ginger beer. And ginger beer drawn from the cask remained for many a memory of the halcyon days of summer long after it had disappeared from the market.

An early recipe for ginger beer recommends boiling the ginger in water, adding sugar, lemon juice and honey, straining the resultant liquor, adding a little egg white and lemon oil and leaving to stand before boiling.

Brewed ginger beers could themselves be alcoholic, whether or not the recipe began, as one did, by taking a quart of brandy. By 1900 the trade press could describe ginger beer as 'the most popular of British non-intoxicating drinks' and it was certainly well regarded as a temperance beverage, but we can only guess whether the popularity was in inverse proportion to the non-intoxication. Nowadays manufacturers produce a more convenient and consistent – and non-alcoholic – drink from a base of ginger-beer essence.

The early commercially bottled lemonades would have used a base of citric acid, described at the time as 'concrete acid of lemons', and essential oil of lemon with a sugar syrup, the mixture being topped up with water and impregnated with carbon dioxide gas. Despite the many technical developments of the intervening years, the lemonades of today are the recognisable successors of the early products.

As these drinks developed during the first half of the nineteenth century, soft drinks outgrew their medicinal origins and their prosperous but hitherto limited clientele expanded to include all ages and classes. The number of makers expanded accordingly. In London alone there were over fifty manufacturers by the 1840s where only ten had been recorded two decades earlier.

This expansion reflected the gradual increase in leisure. It was no coincidence that at the Great Exhibition of 1851 vast numbers of people drank lemonade, ginger beer, Seltzer water and soda-water all supplied by Messrs Schweppes, who paid £5000 for the concession. Wines, spirits, beer and intoxicating drinks were forbidden at the Crystal Palace, being evidently out of keeping with the high purpose of its promoters. As a result over a million bottles of soft drinks were sold, representing almost half the company's production for that year.

But while Schweppes were an up-market range of products, soft drinks were also gaining ground at the other end of the social scale. Costermongers were working the fairs and races with lemonade which they made at home in stone barrels, and at the London markets a wide range of soft drinks was being hawked or sold from stalls to refresh the shoppers. In 1851, according to Henry Mayhew, the customers were chiefly those 'who have a penny to spare rather than those who have a penny to dine upon'.

A costermonger with a barrow load of ginger beer, Clapham Common, London, 1877. On the right is an umbrella mender.

Among the drinkables he noted were ˙tea, coffee and cocoa, ginger beer, lemonade, Persian sherbet, and some highly coloured beverages which have no specific name, but are introduced to the public as "cooling" drinks; hot elder cordial or wine; peppermint water...'

The nature of the drinks with 'no specific name' can no longer even be guessed. Sherbets themselves were by origin cool fruit drinks from the East but the name became attached to effervescent drinks latterly made up from powders consisting largely of bicarbonate of soda, tartaric acid, sugar and flavourings.

At Billingsgate Mayhew heard the hawkers cry 'Glass of nice peppermint, this cold morning a ha'penny a glass!', and at Smithfield 'Ginger beer, ha'penny a glass!' or 'Iced lemonade here! Iced raspberryade, as cold as ice, ha'penny a glass, only a ha'penny!' Mayhew also noted that 'several sellers disposed of their ginger beer in plain glass bottles ... and the liquid was drank out of the bottle the moment the cork was withdrawn, and so the necessity of a glass was obviated.'

Above: *A street seller of sherbet and water for a halfpenny, Cheapside, City of London, 1893.*

Below: *Inside a Victorian soft-drinks factory: filling egg-ended bottles with minimal machinery.*

A full load: Mr E. North (proprietor) and his staff outside North's Soda Water Manufactory, Aylesbury, sometime before 1880.

At the Old Clothes Exchange Mayhew described 'a gaudy-looking ginger beer, lemonade, raspberry and nectar fountain; "a halfpenny a glass, a halfpenny a glass, sparkling lemonade!" shouts the vendor as you pass. The fountain and the glasses glitter in the sun, the varnish of the wood-work shines, the lemonade really does sparkle, and all looks clean – except the owner.' The largest vehicle of the species – at Petticoat Lane – was of mahogany, the proprietor reckoning to take between £7

Cooling drinks! A sherbet seller in Greenwich Park in the 1890s.

and £8 in old halfpennies (that is, 480 halfpennies to the pound) on a fine Sunday morning between six and one o'clock.

In the second half of the nineteenth century mixer drinks developed. By the 1860s brandy and soda was the drink for gentlemen and shandygaff – beer and ginger beer mixed by the publican – was available for heartier thirsts. Already in 1858 Mr Erasmus Bond had produced and patented 'An improved aerated liquid, known as Quinine Tonic Water', which was put on show at the International Exhibition of 1862 with a catalogue entry including a testimonial from a Dr Hassall of Wimpole Street reporting on his analysis of the product and his belief in the benefits to be derived from it.

The origins of ginger ale are more obscure but cannot pre-date the method of producing a clear extract of ginger, since the clarity of the drink is a key feature in distinguishing it from ginger beer. It seems likely, therefore, that ginger ale was first produced in the 1870s and its origins can be traced with reasonable assurance to Belfast. Certainly by 1900 a trade advertisement was asking 'What go-ahead Mineral Water Maker is there who has not at one time or another longed for the day to come when he would be able to turn out a Ginger Ale equal to the world-famous Belfast Ginger Ales?' Nor was ginger ale scorned by those who preferred their soft drinks unadulterated. As a contemporary versifier put it: 'More mellow, more delicious draught, No temperance toper ever quaffed.'

At the end of the nineteenth century hock and Seltzer was still a fashionable mixer. Phil May, the cartoonist, was drawing his 'Scotch and Polly', inspired by the popular drink of the day: Scotch whisky and Apollinaris water from Germany. And in the Café Royal of the 1890s Oscar Wilde was enjoying whisky and soda while Bernard Shaw sipped his Apollinaris water unadulterated.

Left: *Phil May, leading cartoonist of the 1890s, illustrates a popular mixer: a large whisky and a small 'Polly' — Apollinaris water.*

Right: *'The North Pole cannot be reached without lime juice.' Rose's lime-juice advertisement following Dr Nansen's polar expedition of 1895-6.*

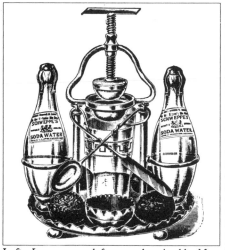

Left: *Lemon squash frame, advertised by Mappin and Webb in 1890: an elegant addition to the temperance dining table!*

Right: *Soft drinks containers: (back, left to right) Codd's bottle with 'marble' stopper; stone ginger-beer bottle (returnable, with fired-on price!); tin-topped siphon; (front) egg-ended bottle for storing on its side, keeping the cork moist.*

BOTTLE-SEALING PROBLEMS

Effective sealing of bottles presented problems from the start. Because the products had a tendency to effervesce, particularly if subject to secondary fermentation, the corks had to be tight or, better still, wired on to the container. Some early bottles were pointed at the base so that they had to be stored lying flat, keeping the corks moist for better sealing.

Ginger beer was especially likely to burst the cork and was bottled in stoneware containers. London schoolgirls skipped to the jingle of 'R. White's ginger beer goes off pop; a penny on the bottle when you take it to the shop!'

Once sealed, opening could be equally difficult. Towards the end of the nineteenth century, the crown cork came into vogue for the smaller returnable bottle still popular today for mixers. While tiger shooting with the Maharajah of Cooch Behar in the 1890s, Lord Frederick Hamilton remarked that the howdahs of the elephants were stocked, *inter alia*, with bottles of lemonade, 'the openers of which were *never* forgotten', clearly a hazard on less well organised excursions.

By the end of the century Hiram Codd's celebrated bottle with the marble stopper in the neck provided perhaps the most ingenious closure ever applied to soft drinks or, as the saying went, to 'Codd's wallop'.

Seltzogenes: early equipment for making carbonated soft drinks at home.

A bottling line for egg-ended bottles, about 1900.

Soda siphons date from the first half of the nineteenth century and even the modern siphon closely follows the design of the late nineteenth century. Until the Second World War siphons were used for a range of mixer drinks and lemonades, not solely for soda-water.

Another ingenious container for domestic use, also relying on the siphon principle for dispensing its contents, was the gasogene, or seltzogene, still occasionally to be seen (empty now) in old curiosity shops.

Filled bottles on an accumulator table awaiting hand-packing, about 1900.

Early dispensing equipment for the fair and fete trade around 1895.

THE STORY UP TO DATE

A glimpse of soft-drinks manufacture around 1900 may today be seen in Mr Bowler's Business at the Bath Industrial Heritage Centre, where J. B. Bowler and Sons' aerated water and cordial factory has been lovingly reconstructed from the original equipment and impedimenta of a firm which appears never to have thrown anything away.

From this and other firms of the period comes a vast miscellany of exotically named products, many of them for the

Left and right: Trade card and price list for J. B. Bowler's 'noted Bath waters' between the world wars.

J.B. BOWLER, CORN S⟨T⟩ BATH.
MANUFACTURER OF ALL KINDS OF
Cordials, Spice Extract, Ginger & Horehound Beer.
ESTABLISHED J·B's NOTED BATH WATERS TRADE MARK 1864 REGISTERED
LEMONADE, GINGER-ALE, BATH PUNCH, QUININE TONIC, SODA AND OTHER AERATED WATERS.

	Per Doz	
SELTZER WATER	2	6
POTASS WATER	2	6
SODA WATER	2	0
SMALL Do.	1	6
LITHIA WATER	3	6
QUININE TONIC	3	0
SMALL Do.	2	0
LEMONADE	2	0
SMALL Do.	1	6
GINGER ALE	2	0
HOREHOUND BEER	2	0
GINGER BEER	1	6
BATH PUNCH	2	0

CORDIALS	Per Bottle	
PEPPERMINT	1	6
CLOVES	1	6
GINGERETTE	1	6
SHRUB	1	6
RASPBERRY	1	6
SPICE EXTRACT	1	0

flourishing temperance movement: horehound beer, cherry ciderette, winter cheer, banana champagne, football stout and quaker pep, not forgetting orange champagne, described in the *Church Times* as 'by many degrees the nicest of its kind'.

In winter, even at a workhouse, Christmas dinner could include lemonade for the children.

On hot summer days grocers prepared cooling drinks by diluting flavoured crystals – lemonade and other powders – to refresh their customers and primitive dispensing equipment was trundled out to fairs and fetes. Thus soft drinks moved further towards instant thirst quenching.

But the production of such bygone beverages was not entirely free from hazard and neither was their consumption, to judge from the following trade advertisement of

A Victorian centenarian testifies to the value of taking the waters.

IF YOU WOULD LIKE TO LIVE LONG FOLLOW THE LEAD OF OUR PICTURED FRIEND AND TAKE THE WATERS OF IPSWICH AS PREPARED BY C·B·KIRBY Mineral Water Manufacturers ST HELENS IPSWICH TEL·503

WELL AND HEARTY AT 101.

THIS IS MRS FRANCIS BAALHAM OF NEEDHAM MARKET AGE 101. HAS TAKEN OUR PURE TABLE WATERS SINCE FIRST INTRODUCED AND IS ONE OF OUR OLDEST CUSTOMERS.

Above: *A small firm's plain and unsophisticated advertisement from a local trade directory of 1905.*

Right: *A statuesque young lady on a 1913 postcard.*

Below: *A musical advertisement from the hop-bitters trade around 1920.*

Ask for
NORTH & RANDALL'S
HIGH CLASS Table Waters.

AYLESBURY,
and at BICESTER.

An art nouveau show card from the early years of the twentieth century.

Loading the carts at Kops yard, Birmingham, around 1900.

1901: 'Caution!! *Arsenic poisoning.* Mineral Water Makers are cautioned against using Acids made by treating calcined bones with vitriol. Phospho-Citric Acid is guaranteed to be absolutely pure and free from all injurious matter.'

Despite such perils the industry and its customers survived and prospered into the twentieth century. Concentrated fruit drinks began to appear. Lime-juice cordial was available well before the new century began. Then an Australian company began

Goodbye to the horse? An early steam wagon, precursor of the heavy goods vehicle.

23

Basic equipment for filling soda-water bottles in a desert campaign of the First World War, 1914-18.

A regimental soda-water factory in the First World War, 1914-18.

Billy Bunter: the well fed schoolboy's enthusiasm for ginger beer survives the passing years.

to put up fruit squashes and concentrated lemon squash was introduced into Britain just before the First World War. In ready-to-drink form, squash had come on to the market by 1890 as a still, cloudy juice-based drink. But the new concentrate gradually annexed the name. After the war orange squash followed, then pineapple and grapefruit. It was in the 1930s that grapefruit as a flavour reached the peak of its popularity.

In the years before the Second World War another popular product crossed the Atlantic: American cola drinks arrived on the British market. As a soft drink, kola with a k was well known in Scotland in the late nineteenth century. In London kola champagne was available in the 1890s and at about the same time kola tonic was advertised as containing 'more nutrient and more capacity for sustaining life than any other natural or prepared article'. The essential flavour of the drink was derived from the kola (or cola) nut, a symbol of hospitality among the Nigerians.

Meanwhile in the United States manufacturers were beginning to market carbonated coca drinks with the flavouring extracted from the leaves of the Bolivian coca shrub, which the natives were accustomed to chew as a stimulant. Then, in 1886, Dr J. S. Pemberton of Atlanta, Georgia, combined the coca and the cola into his celebrated 'brain tonic'. Available in Britain in the 1920s at a few soda fountains

On the beach: a 1930 trade advertisement for soft-drinks bottles.

When Summer comes!

BE prepared by placing your orders now for U.G.B. Mineral Water bottles of Super-Strength and beautiful finish lending character and attractive appearance to your package.
Also Manufacturers of Packing Cases, Van Boxes and Crates of top quality.

U.G.B.
MINERAL WATER BOTTLES.

UNITED GLASS BOTTLE
MANUFACTURERS LIMITED
The largest manufacturers of Glass Bottles in Europe.

Head Offices:
40/43, Norfolk Street,
Strand, London, W.C.2

Above: *Thomas and Evans began to trade direct to the homes of South Wales with their Corona brand in the 1920s.*

Left: *The Corona door-to-door salesman before the Second World War.*

in London's West End, its sales in bottles were modest in the post-Depression 1930s but its popularity took a firm hold once the American troops arrived in the following decade, since when the growth of cola drinks has been assured.

But speciality drinks were by no means all imported. Scotland's second national drink, iron brew, was first made in the early years of the twentieth century and Tizer, the invention of a Manchester man, was successfully promoted as a children's drink in the 1930s and thereafter. Such drinks were usually essence-based, combining various fruit and other flavours to the manufacturer's own particular recipe.

In the First World War the Army had taken considerable pains to ensure the production of soda-water for the troops at the front. The services also encouraged consumption of the new concentrated drinks, more cheaply transported than when ready to drink.

Above left: Scotland's other national drink: a regional favourite in the twentieth century.

Above right: An explanatory advertisement for the unbranded soft drinks sold during the Second World War.

Right: Cartoon by Lee of the London Evening News at the ending of the Second World War in 1945.

In the Second World War the United Kingdom soft-drinks industry itself was subjected to a unique experiment in control. While many products were rationed and others like ice-cream were forbidden, the soft-drinks industry was rationalised: competition was in practical terms eliminated, and a multitude of businesses compulsorily closed. The rest traded not under their pre-war names but as numbered production units, rationed for ingredients, petrol and almost all the other necessities for production and distribution, and selling at prices fixed by the authorities. Profits depended on the ingenuity of the manufacturer in making the most efficient use of what ingredients he could get, a proportion of those profits being shared with the makers who had been forced to close.

After the war many of the closed businesses never reopened. The traditional

" I suppose you're preparing for a rush for Victory Night ? "

The motor lorry enabled the go-ahead manufacturer to deliver further afield: an early vehicle delivering direct to the home.

A direct-supply delivery vehicle of the 1960s.

28

Left: *The anon-ymity of this Second World War return-able SDI (soft drinks industry) bottle is somewhat belied by the branded emboss-ment round the bottom.*

Right: *Show ma-terial for a local bottler in the 1960s.*

horse-drawn vehicle carrying a heavy but inexpensive load traded perforce only in its own locality. Now, speedier produc-tion, mechanised vehicles, lighter packag-ing, all would lead to an ever diminishing band of manufacturers producing a vastly increasing quantity.

Wartime conditions gave a further stimulus to concentrated drinks which was to continue into peacetime. Concentrated blackcurrant juice drinks exploited the vit-amin C available from indigenous sources.

In the 1950s comminuted citrus drinks were introduced and soon rivalled squashes in popularity. Sold as whole-fruit drinks, their flavour was derived not only from the juice but also from the natural oils extracted from the peel as the whole fruit was broken down to provide the basis of the drink.

A low-volume filler for concentrated squashes used during the Second World War and after.

29

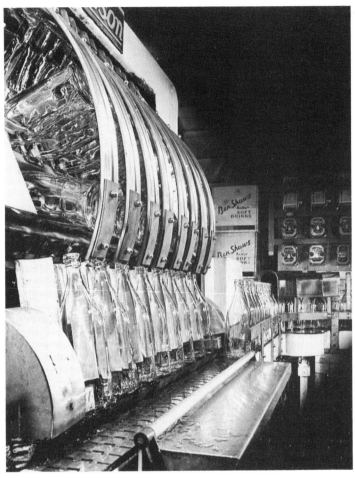

Returnable glass quart bottles being discharged from a giant Dawson bottle washer in the early 1960s.

Another post-war success, bitter lemon, succeeded grapefruit in the flavour range, although popular also as a mixer drink.

Shandy, too, was a post-war success for it was only in the 1960s that Customs and Excise grudgingly allowed the name to be applied to a pre-packed blend of lemonade and beer of final proof-spirit content low enough to be sold lawfully on unlicensed premises.

Low-calorie soft drinks were also introduced in the 1960s, stimulated by new artificial sweeteners which made them more palatable to weight-conscious drinkers.

Packaging, too, diversified, with non-returnable bottles and cans reflecting the supermarket revolution in retailing. Returnable bottles became lighter and standardised, ceasing to carry the ingenious trade-marks and manufacturers' names hitherto embossed in the glass. Draught soft drinks were increasingly found in catering outlets and vending machines reached still more customers. Plastics were adapted for carbonated soft drinks in the form of polyethylene terephthalate or PET for short. The market grew for still soft drinks in cartons, bringing squash back to

Above: *Cases of soft-drinks cans stacked on to a lorry by hand from a fork-lift truck in the early 1960s.*

its ready-to-drink origins.

Bottles became easier to open and to re-seal with the aluminium cap rolled on to the bottle neck. For cans the ring-pull also made opening easier.

The scope of soft-drinks packaging extended to pure fruit juices – first in small glass bottles and later in cartons – and to low- and no-alcohol beers and wines. Spa and spring waters, after languishing for close on two centuries, have also enjoyed a phenomenal expansion in Britain and to some of them, too, flavours have been added.

Thus, from modest and diverse beginnings, soft drinks are now perhaps the most widely sold products of today.

Below: *PET plastic bottles were being produced by blow-moulding in the soft-drinks plant by the 1980s.*

FURTHER READING

Denbigh, Kathleen. *A Hundred British Spas*. Spa Publications, 1981.
Hedges, A. A. C. *Bottles and Bottle Collecting*. Shire, 1975.
Hoy, Ann. *Coca-Cola: the First Hundred Years*. The Coca-Cola Company, 1986.
Searle, Muriel. *Spas and Watering Places*. Midas Books, 1977.
Simmons, Douglas A. *Schweppes: the First 200 Years*. Springwood Books, 1983.
Turner, E. S. *Taking the Cure*. Michael Joseph, 1967.

PLACES TO VISIT

Intending visitors are advised to find out the opening times before making a special journey.

Bass Museum of Brewing History, Horninglow Street, Burton upon Trent, Staffordshire DE14 1JZ. Telephone: 0283 45301. Archives also include artefacts and photographs from soft-drinks companies now incorporated within Bass plc. Special displays drawn from this material are mounted from time to time.

Bath Industrial Heritage Centre, Camden Works, Julian Road, Bath, Avon BA1 2RH. Telephone: 0225 318348. Incorporates 'Mr Bowler's Business', J. B. Bowler's mineral-water factory reconstructed from the copious stock of original artefacts.

Birmingham Museum of Science and Industry, Newhall Street, Birmingham, West Midlands B3 1RZ. Telephone: 021-236 1022. Includes a display of past soft-drinks manufacturing equipment.

Buckley's Museum of Shops, 90 High Street, Battle, East Sussex TN33 0AQ. Telephone: 04246 4269. Includes stone and glass soft-drinks bottles (some still labelled) and show material in displays of a general store, chemist shop and pub bar.

Museum of Advertising and Packaging (The Robert Opie Collection), Albert Warehouse, Gloucester Docks, Gloucester GL1 2EH. Telephone: 0452 302309. Includes a display of bygone soft-drinks containers (some still labelled) and advertisements.

Many regional and local museums contain examples of soft-drinks bygones, particularly glass and stoneware bottles, from past and present soft-drinks manufacturers in the locality.

Old equipment on show at 'Mr Bowler's Business', Bath Industrial Heritage Centre.